Max Adeler

The Tragedy of Thompson Dunbar

A Tale of Salt Lake City

Max Adeler

The Tragedy of Thompson Dunbar
A Tale of Salt Lake City

ISBN/EAN: 9783337073718

Printed in Europe, USA, Canada, Australia, Japan

Cover: Foto ©ninafisch / pixelio.de

More available books at **www.hansebooks.com**

THE TRAGEDY

OF

THOMPSON DUNBAR

A TALE OF SALT LAKE CITY

BY

MAX ADELER

———•———

PHILADELPHIA

J. M. STODDART & CO.

1879

VOTE FOR
THOMPSON
DUNBAR
FOR
MAYOR.

The Tragedy of Thompson Dunbar.

CHAPTER I.

THE ELOPEMENT.

SALT LAKE CITY; the Mormon capital! Let us look at it. It lies deep in the valley, in a valley which is six thousand feet above the level of the sea. To the right, to the left, to the north, the south, the east, and the west, mountains!

Some near, some far. Some mighty, some dwarfed by contrast with the greater. A serrated chain of hills filling the whole horizon and outlining their dusky summits clearly against the pure blue of the sky. From among them the Twin Peaks rise, boldly and grandly, seventy-five hundred feet above the valley, and stand in hoary grandeur, their snow-clad tops the reservoirs from which the plain draws inexhaustible supplies of cold and limpid water. The plain itself, a wide stretch of sandy earth, partly cultivated, but almost wholly covered upon

this August day with myriads of gleaming golden sun-
flowers, which to him who takes a bird's-eye view, seem
a garb altogether glorious.   Lying in the midst of it, the
city.

America has no other like it.   Surveyed from a
distance it wears a distinctly Oriental appearance.   So
we of the Far West who have only dreamed of the East,
imagine how Damascus may look.   White houses shin-
ing amid rich masses of green foliage.   A dome, a tower,
a spire, that may answer for a minaret, deep gardens,
buildings with flat roofs, a faint mist of dust marking the
line of a travelled street, a sky of more than Oriental
softness overhead, and an atmosphere so pure that to
breathe it is luxury, and to look through it is to gain such
power of vision that the peaks of the Wasatch range,
twenty miles away, seem within reach of the pedestrian
who has five minutes to spare.

In the city there are broad streets covered with gravel.
Upon each side where the gutter should be, there is a
stream of pure and delicious water hurtling fiercely along
with the impetus gained at the top of the Twin Peaks.
The dwellings of stone, of wood, of adobe or sun-burned
bricks, are far apart and enshrined among mighty trees.
Shops, here and there, thrust themselves out to the edge
of the footway, and offer their wares to the passers-by.

It is a queer throng that is thus tempted.   Such a
one as no other street in this broad earth can gather.
Here is a Mormon saint, a patriarch with twelve wives,
and so many children that he is compelled to refer to his
memorandum book for a list of them.   Stout, rugged,
coarse in nature and feature, he is of the kind that found

his valley a wilderness and transformed it into a luscious
garden. There is a Utah Indian, clad perhaps in a stove-
pipe hat, a blanket, and buckskin breeches. He wears
huge earrings, long straight hair, thick, and as black as
midnight. Here is a Mexican—dashing along at break-
neck speed, upon a shaggy pony. He wears a dress
as picturesque as that of a Greek, and he is as fine a
horseman as the Arabian desert knows. There go two
army officers, wearing blue coats, and looking as if they
were in authority. They hie to the camp upon the hill
side, from whence the guns that they control can level
the city in a day. Gentile miners, with fierce whiskers.
broad hats, trousers tucked in boots, and pistols thrust in
belts, swagger about in search of firewater; Mormon
policemen, quiet, reserved, but keen as hounds, stand
upon the corners. Huge waggons drawn by six, and
eight, and ten mules come lumbering down the street,
bringing from outlying settlements of the saints the tithes
for the Prophet's storehouse. Hurrying past them, dash
graceful and elegant pleasure carriages such as Hyde
Park might be proud of. But where are the women? Of
men there are enough. Now and then a Gentile woman
passes, but not often ; and the Mormon women appear
still less frequently. It is Orientalism in the extreme
Occident. There is the polygamy of Turkey with an
approach to the custom which keeps the woman under
a veil. It is a strange city, a new city, born within the
last half century ; a city of its own kind ; a city that is as
striking, as novel, as interesting, as unprecedented to the
view of the American who lives east of the Rocky Mountains, as it is to that of the citizen of London.

To begin with. We have to do with a large white adobe structure, which stands upon the eastern edge of the town, in the midst of a garden, wherein are trees that overtop the roof, and grass that is gemmed with flowers. It is Mrs. Ballygag's Boarding School for young ladies. Two young men meet at the gate. We recognize them as young Mormons. One is Thompson Dunbar; the other is Arbutus Jones. Arbutus is speaking.

"Yes, sir; I shall marry them; clean out the school. I have had a special revelation; the entire senior class has been sealed to me, and I am going to marry the two other classes so as to make a complete job of it."

"But the senior and junior classes have engaged themselves to me," replied Dunbar. "I proposed to them yesterday, and they said that they could love me alone."

"Can't help that," said Jones; "I have arranged the matter with the Prophet and the parents. The entire concern has been offered me in marriage, and I am now on my way to see Mrs. Ballygag, and to get her to wind up the term and graduate them at once."

"This is maddening!" exclaimed Dunbar. "Jones, the affections of those classes have been given to me— their young hearts are mine. What right have you to come in and trample rudely upon the holiest emotions of your fellow-creatures?"

"The best of rights, in this case," said Jones. "It has been revealed to me that my duty is to annex this boarding-school. It is a sacred obligation. There is not a bit of use, you know, Dunbar, in your kicking against the decrees of the church."

"But you don't want the whole thirty-two of them?"

"Yes, sir; I want them all. I claim them as my bride."

"I love them all dearly," said Dunbar ; "but sooner than have any fuss I'll let you pick sixteen, if you'll leave me the rest."

"No ; I shall take them all. But I don't know; maybe, I might agree to leave you the one with warm hair and freckles. My heart, somehow, doesn't throb wildly for her."

"Never !" exclaimed Dunbar.

"Oh, very well, then. Let her alone. I'll pool her in with the rest."

The eye of Thompson Dunbar flashed fire. Stepping up to Arbutus Jones, he whispered fiercely in his ear :

"You think you will marry this school. Never! never! I swear it! My faith is pledged to the women of my love, and they shall be mine. Mark what I say! I shall make them my wife !"

Arbutus Jones opened the gate, and, turning away with a light laugh, he said, "Dunbar, don't talk like an idiot," and then he walked up to the porch, pulled the door-bell, and called for Mrs. Ballygag.

Thompson Dunbar sauntered sadly down the street, meditating upon his plans. Secretly he entered his office, and writing thirty-two letters, he dispatched them through the post, and then went towards the livery-stable.

Midnight came. Dark, cold, and silent. The belated wayfarer, walking into town, was startled to perceive, rushing by him in the gloom, a man, who seemed to be carrying a coil of rope upon his arm. Behind him eight carriages proceeded slowly, and with little noise.

" A midnight funeral procession." the traveller thought. The man stopped in front of Mrs. Ballygag's mansion. The carriages halted by the kerbstone, a hundred yards below. The man opened the gate noiselessly, and walked quickly around to the side of the house. He uttered a low whistle, and a sash in a second-story window was carefully raised. He flung toward it the end of a rope, which was seized and hauled until a ladder of rope stretched from the window to the ground.

" Come, dearest." said Thompson Dunbar, in a loud whisper. " Do not be afraid. I will catch you if you fall." Then the form of a lithe and graceful girl emerged from the window, and glided slowly, but easily down the frail ladder. Then another descended. Then another, until thirty-two lithe and graceful girls had reached the ground. As they came, Thompson Dunbar clasped them one by one in his arms, and kissed them fervently, pointing the way to the carriages.

The last one whispered in his ravished ear that the thirty-two trunks were standing, ready packed, in the chamber above, and that Thompson had better see to getting them down. But the idea did not seem to strike Thompson. He asked himself what love had to do with trunks ? He thought how little pure affection cares for material things. He knew that he was ready to die for his darlings. That would be heroic. But to carry thirty-two trunks down a rope-ladder. he considered, in the strictest sense, a prosaic performance. Did Romeo shoulder Juliet's trunk ? Did Paul take Virginia upon one arm, and her trunk upon the other ? Did Petrarch interrupt his sweet converse with Laura with struggles with her luggage? He thought not. Let the trunks remain as a souvenir with Mrs. Ballygag. He gloated over the thought that she and Jones would weep tears of anguish and helpless rage over those leathern receptacles

He went toward the carriages. They were all filled, and the doors were closed. He mounted upon the seat with the driver of the foremost one, and said :—

" Drive like mad, now ! Forty dollars extra for you, if you reach Ogden by daylight ! "

The vehicles dashed onward swiftly through the night. Over rough roads, down through cañons, through dense forests, over mighty hills, along the brow of more than one precipice ; scaring the fox and the rabbit that lay in the path ; waking the echoes of the passes, and defying the winds which blew in gusty blasts from the mountain tops.

It was a long and difficult ride. It would have been tedious for Thompson and his bride, but for the thought that each moment brought them nearer to the wedded bliss which is the holiest joy that has ever sweetened human life.

The day was faintly breaking over the summits of the Wasatch range when the procession entered Ogden. Thompson ordered his companion to drive at once to the house of Bishop Potts. The Bishop's dwelling showed no signs of life. He was asleep with his family—at that early hour. Thompson rang the door bell fiercely. The Bishop's grey head was thrust from the window.

" Who is making all that racket down there ? " he said " What's the matter? What do you want ? "

" It's I, Thompson Dunbar ! I've run over from the

city to be married. Hurry down and perform the ceremony, please."

"Can't you get married at some less unearthly hour
than this? I've been up all night with the twins and
sixteen others of the children, and four of Mrs. Potts have
not had a wink of sleep, and here you come routing us
out just as we are dozing off! I'll marry you after break-
fast.   There is no hurry about it, I reckon."

"But there *is* a hurry though. I've eloped with Mrs.
Ballygag's boarding school.   It loved me, and they
wanted to marry it to another man, Arbutus Jones, you
know; so it fled with me. We are bent on instantaneous
consolidation !"

"How many of her are there?" asked the Bishop.

"Only thirty-two."

"And you're single?"

"Yes."

"Very well.   That'll do to begin with, but a man
of your standing must disembowel a couple more
boarding schools if you want to hold your own in the
church! I'll come down and see what I can do for
you."

Thompson helped his bride to alight, and a most charming picture she presented, standing there in a row in the
early morning light, blushing with modest joy beneath the
smiles and caresses of her devoted lover. While she
waited for the Bishop she engaged in a simultaneous
arrangement of her back hair.   Thompson thought she
had never appeared so lovely as when, holding the front
strands in her mouth, the whole thirty-two of her twisted
up her tresses, and inserted her combs in them.

A moment later the front door opened, and the Bishop appeared in dressing-gown and slippers.

Mr. Dunbar ushered the bride into the Bishop's drawing-room, and seated her upon the sofas and chairs. Then he drew the Bishop aside.

" By the way, Bishop, what are you going to charge? What are your rates?"

" Well," said the Bishop, smiling, " where there is only one couple my regular fee is two dollars. But of course I allow a discount on wholesale transactions. I'll tell you what I'll do. Seeing that you are a young man, and evidently in earnest in your efforts to start properly in life, I'll put you the whole lot in at forty-five dollars. How's that?"

" Reasonable, very reasonable, indeed," said Thompson.

" Stand up, my dear," said the Bishop to the bride.

The bride stood up in a semicircle, while in the doorway gathered seven or eight of the Bishop's wife, to witness the impressive scene.

Thompson Dunbar then advanced, and taking from the pocket of his coat tail a quarter of a peck of gold rings he put them in his hat and handed them to the Bishop, who began the service.

" Thompson Dunbar, you take these women for your wedded wife? You promise to love, honour, and cherish?" etc., etc.

Thompson Dunbar said, " I do."

The Bishop, turning to the bride, said—

" Emma, Henrietta, Louisa, Geraldine, Polly, Mary Jane, Matilda, Gertrude, Lucy, Imogene, Sally, Rebecca,

2

Maria, Georgine. Hetty, Columbia, Martha, Caroline, Patty, Julia, Emily, Anastasia, Rachel, Sapphira, Ethelberta, Hannah, Josephine, Bertie, Mignon, Patience, Agatha, Ann Jane—you take this man to be your wedded husband? You promise to love, honour, and obey?" etc., etc.

And the bride said she did, and she would.

Then Thompson, with gladness in his eyes, and wild emotions in his bosom, took the hat from the Bishop and walked around the semi-circle of the bride, and placed the rings on her fingers. Then the Bishop pronounced them man and wife; and Thompson started around the bridal curve again to clasp her in succession to his heart.

He was just releasing himself from the twenty-sixth clasp when a wild tumult was heard in the street ; the noise of hurrying wheels, the quick tramp of horses, a crying of voices. The Bishop went to the casement to ascertain the cause of the tumult which disturbed the happy marriage festivities. Before he reached the window the door was hurled open with violence, and in rushed Arbutus Jones. Behind him was Mrs. Ballygag.

Jones was white and breathless. Mrs. Ballygag panted, and brandished in a threatening manner a protuberant umbrella.

"Stop! stop!" shouted Jones, as he projected himself into the room. "Don't go on! I forbid the marriage! these women are to be my wife! This man is a depraved villain! I command you, Bishop, not to perform the ceremony!"

"Don't you dare to do it, you grey haired old monster !" shrieked Mrs. Ballygag, menacing him with her umbrella. " You do it at your peril ! "

" I think," said the Bishop, serenely, " you had better try to be calmer. Try to restrain your emotion, as the weather is too warm for violent excitement."

" Let 'em go on," said Dunbar. " It makes no difference if they get their emotional thermometers up to a hundred and ten in the shade; nobody cares."

" You don't care, hey ?" exclaimed Mrs. Ballygag, " you don't care ! I'll make you care if there's any law in the land. Coming round people's houses with rope-ladders in the middle of the night, stealing their poor defenceless children ! I'll see if you don't care !"

" Children, madam ?" said the Bishop.

" Pretty tough children, these !" said Thompson, waving his hand toward the bride.

" Yes, children," replied Mrs. Ballygag, " mere babes and sucklings. Getting married, you baggage !" said she, looking at the bride. " You're in a nice condition to think about marriage ! How do you bound Nova Scotia ? Tell me this instant ! Don't know ? I thought not ! Don't know how to bound Nova Scotia—don't know that the Tropic of Capricorn is not one of the United States ; don't know that the Peloponnesian war was not fought by negroes in Canada West, and yet you consider yourselves fitted for the responsibilities of matrimony ! It's simply too ridiculous to be discussed."

" I am sorry, madam, that they are ignorant of the geographical facts connected with the Peloponnesian war, but we will try to be happy while we study them up together."

"You will *never* study them together," remarked Arbutus Jones   "These ladies return at once with me."

"Certainly!" said Mrs. Ballygag; "they go back to school to-day.   I shall put them on bread and water, and give them fifteen extra sums a-piece in Reduction of Compound Numbers."

"They will *not* go back, I think," said Thompson.

"We'll see about that," replied Jones.   "Girls, leave the room!"

"Don't go!" said Thompson.

"Attend to your own business!" exclaimed Arbutus, fiercely.

"If you speak to me in that manner again, I'll throw you out of the window!" said Dunbar.

"Lay your hand upon me and you are a dead man," replied Arbutus, drawing a revolver.

"Two can play at that game," said Thompson, quickly drawing another.

What the result might have been if the dispute had proceeded further can only be conjectured; but as soon as the weapons were produced, the bride shrieked wildly, and the whole thirty-two of her fell fainting on the floor, while Mrs. Ballygag collapsed, and embracing her umbrella, sank unconscious in the corner.

For a moment, wild confusion prevailed; but the Bishop retained his presence of mind, and running into the garden, he seized a huge watering-pot, and bringing it in, he sprinkled the faces of the bride with water until one by one she revived.   Mrs Ballygag came to without assistance, and sat up looking the picture of distress.

When all of the party were restored, the Bishop said:

"Two can play at that game, said Thompson.—*Page* 20.

"Let us have no more of these scenes! Mr. Jones, it is my duty to inform you that you have come too late. Mr. Dunbar is already married to these ladies."

"Married!" shouted Jones.

"Married!" shrieked Mrs. Ballygag.

"Married," replied the Bishop and Thompson.

"This is infamous," said Arbutus. "Dunbar, you have played me a scurvy trick. But I shall be even with you."

"You can have any satisfaction you want," replied Dunbar. "But, I say, Jones, how about that revelation? Crooked, wasn't it? Didn't reveal so very much after all?"

"We shall see!" exclaimed Jones; and then smashing his hat down savagely upon his head, he left the room.

Mrs. Ballygag began to cry.

"You have treated me shamefully," she said. "The last quarter's bills of these girls are not paid. I can't have any commencement; the reputation of the school is ruined; and I am a poor lone widow-woman, with nobody to help me!"

And Mrs. Ballygag sank down upon a sofa and sobbed violently.

Then the bride began to cry also. It was altogether too melancholy for a wedding. The Bishop drew Thompson aside.

"Dunbar," he whispered, "you'll have to do something for this woman. You must do the fair thing."

"What do you recommend?"

"Well, to tell the truth, if I were you, I'd marry her. just throw her in with the rest, as a kind of job lot. You might as well go the whole figure, while you're at it."

"I suppose I might. I'll take her."

"I'll charge you only twenty-five cents extra for tying the knot," said the benevolent Bishop.

"You propose it to her," said Thompson.

"Mrs. Ballygag," said the Bishop, "how would you like to marry Mr. Dunbar, in with the rest? He says he is willing."

With a wild cry of joy, Mrs. Ballygag rushed forward and threw her arms about Dunbar's neck and nestled her head in his bosom.

"Do you love me, Thompson?" she asked, looking up at him.

"Well, yes; that is, of course, as it were, to a—to a —to a certain extent ! Take your umbrella off my toe, please ; the pressure is too severe !"

"Then take me, take me !" she exclaimed. "I'll help you manage the girls."

The girls looked as if they were not bursting with ecstasy; but they wanted to be submissive to Thompson, and so they said nothing.

Then Dunbar took Mrs. Ballygag by the hand, the Bishop began the ceremony, and in a few moments she was made a thirty-third of him.

CHAPTER II.

THE DEPARTURE.

UPON the homeward journey most of the bride rode in the eight carriages, while the joyous groom occupied his former seat with the coachman of the foremost vehicle. The recent Mrs. Ballygag, however, was compelled by the want of room also to ride with one of the drivers. She entertained him during the journey by a cross-examination, the purpose of which was to ascertain if, in his opinion, a horse is an adverb or a preposition, and if he knew how to multiply vulgar fractions. When he remarked to her, " I ain't got no use for a hymn-book," she parsed the sentence for him, and showed him clearly how two negatives make an affirmative.

Whenever his horses were disposed to go slowly, she prodded them savagely with the ferule of her umbrella, and sometimes when the portion of the bride which was riding in the carriage beneath her laughed too boisterously, she would reach over and push her umbrella in at the window two or three times to indicate her disapprobation of such scandalous behaviour.

Altogether, it is believed that the late widow Ballygag enjoyed the trip exceedingly. But it is doubtful if the driver did ; and it is certain Thompson did not, at least, during the periods when they were passing along the edges of the precipices, and she was constantly screaming for him to come and save her from being dashed to pieces.

At last, however, Salt Lake City was reached, and the bridal party was taken at once to Dunbar's modest little cottage. When the bride had all dismounted and entered the drawing-room, Thompson whispered to the late Mrs. Ballygag that there were four of his wife to whom he had not yet been formally introduced, and he begged her to perform the ceremony. She did so, remarking at the same time to the girls—

"Your husband is a good and worthy man, and I want you to behave well towards him. I am going to keep an eye on you to see that you do it, too!"

The honeymoon passed blissfully. Thompson Dunbar was by profession a sailor, and having no ship at this time he was at liberty to devote himself wholly to domestic life. He purchased new furniture for his house. He made a contract with the calico factory for permanent supplies of dress goods, and the factory at once put in extra looms and employed more hands. He bought bonnets with a recklessness that threatened bankruptcy. He established relations with a candy manufacturer, which guaranteed him the few tons of chocolate drops that he required at lower rates than usual. In fact, he launched himself fairly and equally upon the sea of wedded life.

Wedded life! Ah, how few of us understand those words as they came to Thompson Dunbar and his bride! To how few have they so rich and beautiful a meaning! Many of us think that we have had sweet experiences within the sacred precincts of the home; but not to many of us is it given to have thirty-four souls with but a single thought—thirty-four hearts that beat as one. The man who sits down with one wife by his hearthstone, and thinks he is happy, knows nothing of the tenderer joy of him who, around a hearthstone twenty feet square, gathers thirty-

two sweet faces (the recent Mrs. Ballygag was homely),
and looks love into all of those eyes that speak again.
Such a man has a nobler affection, a loftier aim, a purer
ambition, a mightier impulse to dash into the struggle
of life and win his bread. Who would not toil valiantly
with thirty-three smiles waiting to welcome him home,
and thirty-three hungry women to nourish ?

Thompson Dunbar was proud, and he had a right to
be. Never once in the early days of his married life did
anything happen to cloud his domestic sky ; excepting,
perhaps, on one occasion, when the relict of the lamented
Ballygag hid the kitten in his boot and forgot to tell him
about it ; and never did he have any doubts of the future
excepting when he reflected upon the anguish he should
suffer when his duty should call him away from those he
loved.

And the painful summons came at last.   He was
ordered to join his ship at San Francisco. She was about
to sail upon a three years' cruise. Three years ! It
seemed intolerable to be separated so long from his darlings. Poor Dunbar ! If he could have foreseen the
trials that were in store for him !

The hour of parting arrived. Let us draw a veil over
the scene.   There are some things too sacred for the vulgar eye ; some episodes in a man's life, of which to speak
lightly were a profanation. Mrs. Dunbar clung to him, of
course. Ah, may none of us ever know the agony of such
a farewell. May we never know what a husband suffers
to whom thirty-three wives are clinging in desperate woe.

He tore himself away ! He was gone ! Gone ! And
three groups of eleven each of heart-broken women sank

upon the front steps and sobbed in bitter despair. Then they flew to the windows and gazed after him, and waved their kerchiefs to him, excepting perhaps the aforetime Ballygag, who, in the violence of her emotion, waved a flannel petticoat which she had been mending.

Little did they suspect what they should endure ere they looked upon that fond face again ! Life is so full of disappointments, so full of —— But, however, let us go on.

Thompson Dunbar sailed away upon the bosom of the mighty deep. For some weeks all was well. The treacherous ocean held its powers in leash. One night there was a fearful tempest, and the gallant barque, after a prolonged contest with the elements, sank to rise no more. All on board were lost ; all save one. Lashed to a spar Thompson Dunbar contrived to sustain himself in the seething foam for four days. Upon the morning of the fifth day he was cast upon a desert island. He crawled out of the reach of the waves and fell asleep. He slumbered long, and when he awoke he released himself from the spar, and looked about him. He perceived that the island was small. It was only fifteen feet wide by thirty-eight feet long ; but Dunbar was satisfied with it. It was something for him to stand upon, to live upon.

Feeling hungry, he walked out looking to find something to eat. He discovered a bed of fine oysters in a little cove at the northern end of the island, and to his great joy he found that a huge hole in the rock contained a dozen hogsheads of rain water ! These things were so exceedingly fortunate that he felt sure of going through the regular round of desert island experiences. But in

this he was, to a certain extent, disappointed. The oysters and water remained, of course, and now and then some sociable bird would call and leave an egg, but none of the usual desert island conveniences floated ashore.

Thompson Dunbar remained upon the island for fifteen years ; but when his clothing began to wear out no vessel was wrecked upon an adjacent and handy reef, and all the crew drowned, so that he could have a fair chance at the chests which contained clothing that fitted him exactly.

And no other ship was cast ashore into which he entered and found twenty bags full of Spanish doubloons, which he gazed at with proud contempt, while the thought occurred to him how useless such dross is, especially when you are on a desert island, with no possibility of spending it.

And he did not find in the cabin of such a wreck double-barrelled guns and carpenter's tools, and canned fruits and vegetables, and such a general variety of useful and fancy articles as no ship ever included in a single cargo, excepting perhaps in cases where the purpose of the owners was to have been wrecked to oblige some Robinson Crusoe or other, and to make him fat and comfortable.

And when he felt lonely and longed for fellowship and the sweet communion of some kindred soul, it did not happen that a squad of chocolate-coloured cannibals dashed up in a canoe, and were all killed by a single explosion of a musket ; all save one, who fell at Dunbar's feet, and became his slave and his pupil and his riend.

On the contrary, Dunbar had a particularly prosaic time upon the island; eating and sleeping and walking about. After the first shock produced by his sense of isolation had passed, he surveyed the island and made a map of it. Then he took possession of it in the name of his government, and formally annexed it to the United States by hoisting a flag made of a felicitous combination of his handkerchief and his red flannel shirt. In order to put in the time, and to give himself occupation congenial to an American, he held elections thrice a year, and he celebrated the 4th of July and Washington's birthday, when they came around, by reading the Declaration of Independence, and singing the " Star Spangled Banner."

But his wife! Did he ever think of her? Ah, yes! The bitterness of that separation no tongue can tell. Often he would lie upon his back and take from his pocket the thirty-three miniatures and look at them with longing and tearful eyes. And he would get to wondering which was Emma, which was Rebecca, which Columbia, and which Sapphira. The lineaments of Ballygag were the only ones he felt certain about, but, somehow he never lingered very long over them.

And he would ask himself if any of her ever thought much of him. He would wonder if she was all alive, or if, perchance, some of her counted him dead, and had remarried. Perchance she had departed, sorrowful and broken-hearted, and only thirty-three little grassy mounds in the churchyard remained to mark the remains of her who once had been the joy of his life.

It might be that if he should ever return home he

"Often he would lie on his back and take from his pocket the thirty-three miniatures and look at them."—*Page* 29.

would find his cottage desolate, with no one to love, none to caress, and it would devolve upon him to begin life afresh by embezzling another boarding-school. The thought was bitterness to him. Only those who have learned from a sad experience what it is to lose three and-thirty wives at a blow, can realize the depth and intensity of the sufferings of this unhappy young man.

CHAPTER III.

THE VICTORY OF JONES.

MEANTIME, how did Mrs. Dunbar bear the bereavement that had come to her? For the first three or four years she was hopeful; but gradually, as the time passed swiftly by, and no word came to her from the wanderer, she began to feel the growing agony of despair.

Often she would go up as the evening shadows fell, and stand at each of the thirty-three windows, and gaze out toward the glowing west, straining all sixty-five of her eyes (Ethelberta had a cataract), to catch a glimpse of her Thompson. But, alas! Thompson did not come; and as a feeling of deep sadness stole in over her souls, Mrs. Dunbar would bow her heads over the infants in her arms and weep. Perhaps she would wail out her woes in a plaintive lullaby, which was so distorted by her sobs that Ballygag's former partner would stop long enough to scold her for singing flat, and not marking the dotted notes with sufficient distinctness.

The misery of a suffering woman's heart! Who shall

sound it? And what multiplication table can compass it where it is thirty-three times increased? There are some conundrums that have to be given up at the outset.

At last, however, she was forced to the conclusion that Thompson was dead. It was inevitable. The ship had never been heard from. No message had ever come up from the roaring sea, to tell the story of her destruction. She was gone; and, without doubt, Thompson had gone down fathoms deep into the cruel waters with her. Mrs. Dunbar abandoned hope, and decided to mourn for him as one that had been called away to another life.

As soon as her determination became known, and she began to talk about putting on mourning the city merchants noted an advance of two per cent. in crape and black bombazine, and the bachelor Saints began to have revelations concerning their duty to persuade her from prolonging the period of her widowhood.

Arbutus Jones was enabled to perceive with perfect clearness, what were his obligations in the premises. He made up his mind that the anguish of Mrs. Dunbar could be assuaged only by sweet words of consolation from his lips. He called early to offer his sympathies, and afterwards he would go around often in the evenings and talk with her about the virtues of the departed Thompson, for whom, however, it was impossible for him to feel any but a fictitious enthusiasm.

After a while, he became more assiduous in his attentions, and he felt, reviving in his bosom, with all its vehement force, the love he had for her when she was maidens. Often he would lead her forth in the twilight, and, while as many of her little hands as he could conveniently

" While as many of her little hands as he could conveniently hold, lay
confidingly in his."—*Page* 32.

3

hold, lay confidingly in his, they would stroll to some quiet, grassy dell, and she would arrange herself in a circle by the side of a babbling brook, while he sat in the centre, and whispered soft words of love to her, and walked around, and pressed each of her hands, and let the love light of his eyes shine on her faces, and warm to life the flickering flame in her hearts.

One evening he proposed to her in a lump. He asked her to be his. The Ballygag was the first to speak. She said :—

"Have you examined your heart, Arbutus? Do you love us truly?"

"Certainly! Of course! Most of you, anyway. However, sooner than lacerate your feelings, I am willing to count *you* out, and permit you to cling to the memory of Thompson."

"But I'm the one that can't be counted out. If you love me, I am yours!"

"I am willing to sacrifice my love for your sake, to save your feelings."

"You are too noble," said the late Mrs. B. "I cannot consent to such an act of heroic devotion upon your part."

"I think you would be happier, maybe, without me. I'll start you in another boarding-school."

"Loving heart! And do you think I would be willing to accept such unselfish kindness, when I could not repay you by watching over you? Never!"

"And then you know," said Jones, "Dunbar might eventually turn up and it would be so comforting for him to have at least one of his wives remaining to him. So

upon the whole, perhaps, I had better let you float along
as you are."

"Ah! Arbutus! I love you more than ever when you
show yourself so ready to surrender your own joy for the
good of others. Take me, oh take me to your fond
bosom!"

And the former Mrs. Ballygag fell towards him with a
purpose to be folded to his heart; but Jones, with remark-
able presence of mind, pretended not to see her, and
addressed himself assiduously to the task of assisting
Sapphira to rise from the ground. Then the whole of
Mrs. Dunbar rose, and retiring a little space, went into
committee to consider the question. After an animated
debate, during which the Ballygag gave her views the
fullest and most generous expression, Mrs. Dunbar
decided by a vote of twenty-nine to three (the woman
with the cataract not voting) to become the wife of Arbutus Jones!

Jones learned the decision with transports. One by
one his sweetheart was held in his fond embrace, as he
kissed her and promised to be true to her; and one by
one, as she looked into his manly face and found there
the radiant joy of pure affection, she was filled with trust-
fulness and peace, and with him went back to her home
full of blissful anticipations of a future which should com-
pensate for all the suffering of the sorrowful past.

Mr. Jones was very anxious to be married speedily;
but the widow, of course, pressed for such delay as would
be necessary to enable her to prepare new outfits of
clothing. There are always stirring times in the business of a community when a Mormon wife or widow

begins to make a movement in the matter of clothes. In this case, the appearance of Mrs. Dunbar unexpectedly in the market, caused such a revival in trade, that the merchants began to buy houses and lots, and to set up carriages under the impression that a new era of prosperity had begun. But eventually Mrs. Dunbar was ready, and the day was fixed. She expressed a preference for Bishop Potts, of Ogden, as the officiating clergyman, because she was used to him, and, of course, Jones asked the worthy Bishop to come over and tie the knots.

The wedding attracted a good deal of attention in Salt Lake City. Jones sailed up the aisle of the temple with Sapphira and Ethelberta upon each arm, while fifteen of his best friends each convoyed two others of .Mrs. Dunbar. The sexton brought up the rear with the ex-widow Ballygag, who honoured the occasion by turning out in a green bonnet with yellow ostrich feathers, a crimson poplin dress embroidered with blue, with a new false front upon her head, and with a look of beaming happiness bursting through her gold spectacles.

The ceremony occupied but a few moments, and when the Bishop having made these thirty four one flesh, the procession turned, passed down the aisle again, entered the carriages, and went to the home that was once Dunbar's, but now had come into the possession of Jones.

Dunbar! how he would have been torn with agony if he, far away upon that lonely island of the sea, could have witnessed that scene in the temple! But this torture was mercifully spared him. At the moment when his loving wife was given to another by the Bishop,

Thompson was splitting oysters open with his jack-knife, and thinking how uncommonly good they would be with horse-radish. No voice whispered the truth to him. No pangs of the heart interfered with the vigour of his gastric juice !

Of the domestic life which came to Arbutus Jones, with the golden days which followed the wedding, we need not speak. It passed away sweetly and brought him perfect contentment. But one day, a month or two after the marriage, Arbutus, upon his return home, found an elderly lady whom he did not know occupying a seat at his dinner-table. He thought at first it might be one of his wife, so he counted the row of her, and found that there were thirty-four women instead of thirty-three. A moment later Sapphira introduced the stranger as her mother.

"She has come to stay with us. Arbutus, dear, upon my invitation. I longed to have her with me, and I knew you would welcome her for my sake. Won't you, darling ?"

"Oh, certainly ! Glad to see her ! Very glad ! Of course. She is always welcome here !"

But Jones did not look as if he were really glad. A dark foreboding entered his mind. The precedent was bad ; it was dangerous. If this kind of thing began, where was it going to stop ? That was the question that he asked himself, with gloom in his soul and a scowl upon his brow.

Two days later Mary Jane's mother arrived. Mary Jane said that she had invited her mother down to spend the summer, and to give her a chance to learn to her son-in-law. Arbutus forced a smile as he welcomed her, but it was not difficult to see that his mother-in-law would have to labour hard to induce him to return her love.

The following week Ethelberta's mother came, ostensibly for the purpose of superintending an operation upon Ethelberta's cataract. But Arbutus saw plainly through the pretence. He was far too acute a man not to know that a woman who comes for the purpose of witnessing an operation upon a cataract is not necessarily accompanied by six trunks, eleven boxes, a bedstead, two bureaus, a sewing-machine, a cooking-stove, a poll parrot, and a cat. She had come to stay. He knew it, and he grated his teeth as he strove to bear it patiently.

A month passed, and at intervals mothers-in-law continued to arrive, until there was a sum total of twenty-one in Jones's house. He began to grow desperate. One day he called the Ballygag aside. He asked her if she had a mother. She said she had not.

Arbutus clasped her in his arms and kissed her tenderly. She was amazed. He had not been lavish of caresses with her. She asked for an explanation. He said—

" I adore a woman who has lost her parents. Ah, Lucille !" (her name was Lucille), " my only regret now is that you didn't keep an orphan asylum instead of a boarding-school, when Dunbar eloped with your establishment."

As he spoke thus the door-bell rang. Lucille went out to see who was there. When she returned, she said the mothers of Columbia and Emma had just arrived with two waggon-loads of trunks and furniture.

Arbutus shuddered.

"This is terrible, Mrs. Bally—Lucille, I mean. If this thing continues I shall go mad. I did not bargain for this. Twenty-three of them already— twenty-three mothers-in-law ! My reason will totter on its throne !"

"Yes," said the former Mrs. B., "and Henrietta and Sarah and Matilda told me that they had written this morning for their mothers to come on and live here; and Sarah said she had invited one of her aunts also."

A spasm of pain flitted over the face of Arbutus Jones. He sat down upon a chair. Was the curse come upon him? Were the fates preparing for him a scorpion whip of retribution for his destruction of Dunbar's hopes of happiness? We cannot tell. Maybe we wouldn't tell if we could.

While he sat there trying to think what he should do to avert the calamity that was overpowering him, a servant entered with a telegram. Jones tore it open and read it.

"Wh—wh—what's this ? ' My dear son-in-law : Meet me at the train on Tuesday. I am coming to board with you for a few months. I am your affectionate mother-in-law.—'REBECCA FITLER.'

"Rebecca Fitler! Who—what—which one's she?"

"She is Imogene's mother. I know her well. She's worse about a house than the whooping-cough. Quarrelled with her husband till she killed him," said Lucille.

"Ha! ha!" laughed Jones, fiercely. "Twenty-six mothers-in-law and an aunt! This is refreshing! It is delightful! Lucille, I am beginning to feel murderous!

If this kind of thing goes on I shall soon be in a frame of mind which will make indulgence in assassination seem like pastime."

" I'm afraid it *will* go on," said the late Mrs. Bally-gag, looking out of the window ; " I see Geraldine's mother coming up the front yard with a carpet-bag and a band-box. She makes twenty-seven ! "

" Twenty-seven and an aunt! " exclaimed Arbutus. " Five more to hear from ! But we can rely upon them to come, I think, can't we, Lucille ? May be I'd better write to them for fear they forget it ; " and Arbutus laughed a wild, hysterical laugh.

" What are you going to do about it ? " asked the late widow B.

" Do? What am I going to do? I am going to do something terrible ! Something desperate ! No man can stand this persecution ! I don't mind having a couple of dozen or so of mothers-in-law around, but the line must be drawn somewhere, and I draw it at twenty-seven and an aunt."

" You could get rid of them by obtaining a divorce," said Lucille.

" No ; I shan't do that. It's too expensive. Besides, I don't want to give up the girls."

" Suppose you order the mothers to leave, and if they refuse force them from the house ? "

" Won't do," said Arbutus, shaking his head thought-fully. " You don't know them. An army couldn't put them out—an army rigged out with Krupp guns and battering rams. No, no ! We must resort to something more desperate."

"How would it do to put poison in their tea?"

"I can't see any profit in it. They'll die. I'll have to stand the funeral expenses, and may be pay the cost of the *post-mortem* examinations."

"Well, then, blow them up with gunpowder."

"No, dear; you must suggest something more practicable. The explosion would disfigure the furniture, and it would make old Partridge, the coroner, wild with joy. Lucille, I hate that man with bitter hatred; and shall I do a thing that will give him thirty or forty inquests, and help him to pay off the mortgage on his house? Never, my dear, never!"

"I don't see how we can manage it, then," said the Ballygag.

"Let me give you an idea," said Arbutus. "I have in my mind the outlines of a malignant plot, which will rid me of these women for ever. It is an awful thing to do, this that I propose, but the case is desperate; I am driven to an extremity. Will you promise to help me in it?"

"Yes."

"Do you know any of Mrs. Brigham Young."

"Oh, yes; one of her went to school to me. She was the best girl I had at grammar. She could tell a participle as far as she could see it."

"Well," said Arbutus, "I want you to go to see her. Tell her I will give her a thousand dollars if she will persuade the Prophet to have a revelation declaring that all my mothers-in-law must be sealed at once to Partridge, the coroner! Will you?"

"You must have a very deep grudge against Partridge.'

"I have! I want him to suffer. Will you go?"

"I will; and I think I can manage the matter for you. How about Sarah's aunt?"

"Run her in with the rest! Make it as hard for Partridge as we can. Give him the whole twenty eight."

"I'll go around at once," said Lucille, and she left the room.

A gleam of savage exultation shone from Jones's eyes, as he thought of the probable completeness of his vengeance. In an hour the Ballygag returned. It was all fixed. She had a promise that the order would be issued the next morning.

Sure enough, next morning Partridge called, looking livid with rage.

"Where," said he to Jones, "are these preposterous old hags that you are trying to shove off on me? Where are they? Trot 'em out so's I can see 'em."

"See here, Partridge, I don't want you to speak in that disrespectful manner of my wife's mothers. What do you want to see them for?"

"Oh, you needn't pretend you don't know. I'm mighty certain you fixed this thing up against me. But I s'pose I've got to take 'em. So let's see 'em."

The ladies filed in. Jones announced the news to them, as gently as he could. Six fainted on the spot. Ten simply screamed. Three said they'd die rather than marry a coroner. Three, and Sarah's aunt, smiled, and said they considered it as, upon the whole, rather a good thing.

"Well, I don't," replied Partridge. "To speak plainly you're a discouraging-looking crowd. See here, you women who are screaming there, you needn't carry on in that manner. You don't want me any less than I want you !"

" Partridge," said Jones, "go about it with more suavity. You can't possibly gain their affection if you proceed in that manner. Woo them gently."

" I don't want any interference from you," replied Partridge. " Here, you women! Get on your things, and come along. I'd commit suicide to get rid of you, if it wasn't that I don't want my successor to collect a fee for my remains. Come on now, and be quick about it."

Then the bride and groom filed out; Mrs. Jones, meantime, standing in a line in the hall weeping, while Jones kept his handkerchief to his eyes and chuckled.

When Partridge reached the front gate, he turned around, and, shaking his fist at Jones, he shouted :—

" You never mind ! I'll pay you for this, old fellow ! "

And then the party proceeded to the temple, and soon was hopelessly bound in the chains of wedlock.

Upon the departure of his wife's mothers, Jones rubbed his hands, and, in a gleeful mood, danced about the room with the Ballygag. He was joyful. He had reason for joy. But there was a dire and awful retribution preparing for him. The shadow of his doom was slowly creeping toward him.

CHAPTER IV.

THE RETURN.

FIFTEEN years had elapsed since Thompson Dunbar tore himself away from his bride, and his happy home. Fifteen years had he dragged out a dreary existence upon his lonely rock in the midst of the sea. One day he saw a ship approaching the island, and he made frantic signals to attract the attention of those on board. Twice the ship seemed to turn away from him, but at last, to his great joy, his signals were answered, a boat was lowered, and in half-an-hour he stood upon the deck of " The Golden Horn," bound for San Francisco.

The captain gave him a suit of clothes, and loaned him some money ; and as soon as the vessel touched the wharf, a few weeks later, he leaped ashore, and took the first train for Salt Lake City.

Imagine the alternations of hope and despair that distracted his mind ! Again and again he asked himself how he should find her. Would she be all alive and well, or partially dead ? Would his children be alive ? Would he find his home as beautiful as ever ? Would he go there to obtain peace and joy, or to suffer pangs of terrible sorrow ?

As he mused, the train entered the city. It was early afternoon. He thought he would go to the hotel and learn something of the truth, before he sought his cottage. It might be less terrible if he should be prepared beforehand.

The landlord of the hotel did not recognize him.

His bronzed and furrowed face, his shaggy hair and beard, his bent form, suggested nothing of the Thompson Dunbar who had gone away a decade and a half before.

Thompson sought information from the landlord.

"Did you know a man named Thompson Dunbar?" he asked.

"Yes, indeed! Knew him well. He left here fifteen or sixteen years ago. He was a sailor, you know."

"What became of him?"

'Lost, sir, lost! It's supposed so, at any rate. No word ever came from him, or about him. His ship was wrecked, we know."

"Was he married?"

"Married! Ah! that's just it, sir! He was married to thirty-three of the loveliest girls in the city. A young and charming bride, and a swarm of the dearest children."

"Did Mrs. Dunbar take it hardly?"

"Indeed she did, sir! Cried her eyes out, nearly. Went on at a most fearful rate. Everybody sympathized with her."

"Is she all alive yet?"

"Oh yes."

"And well?"

"I believe so; perfectly. She was the last time I saw her."

"When did you see her?"

"Well, I haven't seen her myself for several weeks; but my book-keeper told me he saw three of Mrs. Jones out driving yesterday."

"I was referring to Mrs. Dunbar," said Thompson.

"I know," replied the landlord ; "I say my clerk saw three of her riding out."

"But you said he saw Mrs. Jones."

"Well, don't I say he saw Mrs. Jones! You seem to be dull of comprehension."

"Maybe I am ; maybe I am. Only you are talking about Mrs. Jones, and I am talking about Mrs. Dunbar."

"But, my goodness man! See here! Her name *was* Dunbar when she was Dunbar's wife, wasn't it? And when she married Jones her name was Jones. Do you understand?"

"Married! is she married?"

"Certainly! of course!"

"Married to Jones! What Jones?"

"Why, Arbutus Jones; been married several years.'

The head of Thompson Dunbar fell upon the table, and he did not even try to keep back the sobs which burst from his overladen heart. Then a thought occurred to him. Looking up he said to the landlord :—

"And Jones? He is dead?"

"No, sir ; alive and well, and heartier than ever."

Thompson Dunbar arose and staggered from the room. He sought the privacy of his chamber, where he could weep tears of passionate grief.

An hour or two later his mind was made up. His heart was broken, but he would have one long, last lingering look at his darlings and his children before he sought the tomb.

He seized his hat and cane, and walked rapidly toward the house where he used to live. As he came near to it he recognized it as the old place but little changed. How dear it had been to him! How much he had loved it! And now another polluted its hearth-stone. Another had whitewashed its fence! He groaned as he thought of these things.

There were children playing in the yard. One hand-some boy had run out into the highway after an errant ball. Thompson spoke to him. The boy stopped to listen. Thompson recognized the suit he had on. It had been made by a pious maternal hand from Dunbar's own wedding coat.

Thompson asked the boy to sit upon the grass with him.

"What is your name, my lad?" he asked.

"William T. Dunbar, sir," the boy replied.

"And where is your father?"

"Drowned!"

"Are you sure of that?"

"Yes, sir. I know he is. Mother says so."

"Have you no other father?"

"Yes! old Jones!"

"Do you love him?"

"No, sir; not when he licks me."

"He whips you, does he?"

"Sometimes!"

Dunbar felt his anger growing hot. He felt an im-pulse to go in and kill Jones on the spot; but he thought better of it.

"What would you say, my dear boy," he asked, "if I should tell you that your real father is not dead?"

"I should say you were a scandalous old story-teller."

"But I do tell you so! I am your father!"

The boy laughed, when he looked thoughtfully at
Dunbar and said:—

"Did you ever read the story about George Washington and his little hatchet?"

"Yes, my son."

"Well, you'd better go home and study up that story.
George couldn't tell a lie.   There'll never be an anecdote
of that kind written about you."

Thompson heaved a deep sigh.   He was about to
reason with the lad, when a sharp female voice was heard
calling—

"Billee—ee—ee—ee—ee!   Billee—ee—ee!"

"That's me!" said the boy.   "She's calling me.   I
must go," and he jumped from the ground.

"Who is it?" asked Dunbar.

"Old Ballygag, we call her," said the boy.   "One of
pa's wives!"

The next moment the head of Ballygag was projected
over the fence top, and she saw Thompson.

"Billy," she exclaimed, "you come into the house
this instant!   How many times have I told you not to
have anything to do with those abominable tramps that
come loafing about here, sneaking little children away
from their parents, and breaking their mother's heart.
You'll be kidnapped the first thing you know, or lost
like your poor dear father, who went down to the bottom
of the Pacific Ocean and was never heard of again,
leastways, by any of us who ought to have heard of him
if he was alive and well, which he wasn't, Heaven bless
his soul! for how could he be when he was bitten all to
pieces by the sharks?   Billy, come right in this minute;

" Billy, come right in this minute."—*Page* 48.

and you, you old vagabond, move on, and don't come
hanging around here looking like a long-haired lunatic,
scaring people's children half to death! Move on, or I'll
call the police!"

And the Ballygag grasped Billy, already upon the
other side of the fence, boxed his ears a couple of times
and led him in bawling.

Thompson turned sadly away and began to walk towards his hotel. A tramp! And this was a woman he
had once called by the endearing name of wife! Better
to have stayed upon his desert island and to have died
there miserable and forlorn, than to have come home to
such agony and insult as this.

He determined never to seek his home again unless
he should resolve to reveal himself to his wife. But the
yearning that he felt was too strong. He could not resist
it. When the shadows of evening fell he sought the
house again. There were brilliant lights in the windows
as he softly crept through the gateway and trod with
noiseless footfall upon the gravelled walk. He stepped
upon the porch, and hiding behind a shutter he peered
through the casement.

How beautiful that sweet domestic scene! but how
horrible for him! His own dear sitting-room, and yet not
his!

There she was! Emma, Sapphira, Ethelberta, Henrietta, Columbia—all of her. A few of her sat about the
centre table knitting. A few of her, were ranged around
the wall. Lucille (his own Ballygag) was there making
over one of Thompson's shirts for Jones! Everything
seemed to conspire to cut him up.

There was Arbutus Jones, his old rival, sitting in an arm-chair with smiling face, dandling three infants upon each knee. He was playing with them and with forty-two other children; and in a corner were seven cradles full of babes, among them two twins and a triplet, which were rocked by a hydraulic engine operated by pellucid water from the sparkling mountain stream. Every now and then one of Mrs. Jones would look up from her work and smile at her husband and at the pranks of the little ones. They were all so peaceful, so happy, so thoughtless of the haggard man who shivered and shuddered out there in the dusky night as with wild eyes he devoured the scene.

Thompson looked eagerly at the children. In the faces of some he traced his own lineaments, his own noble Roman nose; in others he saw distinctly the facial outlines of Jones : he saw the nose which turned upward as if perpetually it would sniff the celestial constellations.

There was a great pain in his heart. He did not know what to do. He was dazed, bewildered. His first impulse was to express his emotion by bursting in the window with a brick. But he repented him of the thought. His wife was happy. It would be most horrible for him to break in upon the even current of her lives and to bring misery to that joyous household. He could not bear to do it. What right had he to make Jones's children mother-less, and their father a houseless wanderer? He would not do so fearful an act. He would go quietly away and lay him down and die. Death would be welcome to him now. He had nothing to live for, nothing to hope for, no joy or happiness any more in this cold and cruel world.

He returned again to his lodging. That night a

raging fever attacked him. For days he was wild with delirium, but at last the fever left him, and he became conscious. His life was fast ebbing away. The physician told him that the end was near. He must finish at once his connection with the affairs of this world.

He called for his landlord.

"When I am dead," he said, "I want you to have my remains prepared for the tomb, and then I wish you to send for Mrs. Arbutus Jones to come here to look upon my face."

"Which of her?" asked the landlord, sadly.

"All of her. She loved me once. She will wish to see me."

"Who are you?"

"THOMPSON DUNBAR!"

And then his tired spirit winged its way into the illimitable ether. He was no more. Perhaps he was even less.

The last message of the unhappy Thompson was conveyed to Mrs. Jones ; and she came, in melancholy array, to view all that remained of him who had won the love of her youth. It was a sad, sad scene at that reunion. Thirty-two fond women in tears, and the late Mrs. Ballygag haunted by an awful fear that she had slain him by denouncing him as a tramp, snatching his boy from his arms, and driving him from his home.

Even Jones was affected. Overcome by the spectacle of his wife's grief, he wandered off disconsolate to the barroom, and tried to find solace in a variety of mixed beverages.

Of course Coroner Partridge came ; his duty was to view the body. When the shocking story was told him, he laughed. Partridge, a man holding a high and responsible and most solemn public position actually laughed boisterously. Persons thought that his familiarity with woe had robbed him of sensibility ; but that was not it. Partridge had suddenly thought of a terrible scheme of revenge.

The funeral was held upon the following Tuesday. Mrs. Jones attended in full force, and each of her carried with her a modest tombstone, bearing a tribute to the memory of Thompson Dunbar. They buried him upon the hillside with impressive ceremonies, and then Mrs. Jones planted the thirty-three tombstones upon the grave and watered them with her tears.

Mrs. Jones returned to her home sorrowful, but trying to regard the matter with a spirit of resignation. Thenceforth she would be happy with her children.

Happy ! The next morning Mr. Partridge called. Mr. Jones and the whole of his wife were at home. After some preliminary and original remarks about the weather, Partridge said—

" By the way, Jones, you know my brother Joe ?"

" The druggist, you mean ?"

" Yes, the druggist. I called, ladies, to ascertain what you think of him."

" We don't know him," the ladies said.

" And we don't want to know him," Jones added.

" Ah, that is indeed unfortunate. I hoped the ladies knew him and admired him," said Partridge.

" Nobody," replied Jones, sarcastically, " admires a man who looks like a clothes-pin stuck in an apple. That isn't our favourite style of man."

"How sad!" exclaimed Partridge, calmly. "It would be so much better for all parties if there was some basis upon which to build a genuine affection."

"Affection! What in thunder do you mean?" demanded Jones, warmly, and rising from his chair.

"Why," said Partridge, "where parties have to live together, love is necessary to happiness."

"Partridge!" exclaimed Jones, "I don't want to knock out your brains ; you have so little to spare. But I shall be obliged to do so if you keep on. I'll brain you right before Mrs. Jones"

"Mrs. Jones!" said Partridge. "What Mrs. Jones? I don't see any Mrs. Jones about here."

"No more of this nonsense," said Jones, fiercely. "Quit now, or I'll throw you out of the window."

"When I quit, these ladies go with me," said Partridge, waving his hand toward the group.

"Mr. Partridge, please explain your self," appealed Sapphira

"Certainly, madam."

"He'd better, or I'll murder him," said Jones.

"I suppose, ladies, you consider yourself the wife of this person, Jones?"

"Certainly," was the unanimous answer.

"Of course," shouted Jones.

"Well, you ain't," said Partridge.

"Why not ?" they asked.

"You were married to him while Dunbar was alive. The marriage, therefore, was illegal. It was null and void. Consequently, you are now simply Mrs. Dunbar, the widow of the late Thompson Dunbar."

"Is that all," said Jones, laughing; "we'll soon remedy that. We will perform the ceremony again this afternoon."

"Oh, no you won't, Mr. Jones," sneered Partridge. "I don't think you will."

"Why not? I'd like to know who will prevent me?"

"I will."

"How?"

"Last night, the Prophet Young had a revelation. He was commanded to seal the whole of the widow Dunbar to another man. That man was my brother Joe!"

Arbutus Jones uttered a wild exclamation, which can-not be reproduced here without injury to good manners and to the morals of the reader. The thirty-three widows fell fainting upon the floor. Partridge sent a servant to call up his carriages. They came. Jones showed some signs of a resistance, but Partridge said :—

"Come, now, old fellow, you know it's of no use. This is exactly the way you played it on me, and I took my punishment like a man. You might as well do the same. Joe 'll make her a better husband than you, any-way."

Jones perceived the folly of fighting against the Prophet and fate. He kissed his darlings fondly, as they began to resuscitate, and then flying out into the garden, he sought a deep recess among the trees, and cursed Joe and all the Partridges, and the Prophet, and the Church, and Mormondom generally, from Joe Smith down to Brigham, and back again. Then he left his home for ever. envious of the rest that had come to his rival, Dunbar, in the depths of the sepulchre.

Partridge took the widow down to his brother Joe's, and Joe and he tried to persuade her to accept her fate. She did so, at last, sullenly and reluctantly ; but, nevertheless, with recognition of the fact that it was a religious duty. She was married to Joseph Partridge, and to his home she came after the ceremony. He tried to make her happy by giving her free run of the gum drops, and liquorice, and jujube paste, and fancy soap, and tooth brushes in the store. But none of these things comforted her, and life became more intolerable for her every day.

Jones did call one day, when her husband was away on business at Ogden, and proposed to her to elope with him, and join the Gentiles. But none of her were willing to commit such an awful sin, excepting the high-spirited and irrepressible Ballygag ; and Jones, after considering the matter, concluded that the enterprise, in her company, had not those fascinating characteristics which had seemed to him to distinguish it when the idea first occurred to him. He bade the whole of Mrs. Partridge farewell, for ever, and, going out into the wilderness, he foreswore civilization. He joined the Kickapoo Indians, and began practising war-whoops.

As for Mrs. Partridge, she dwindled and died, one by one, and her husband bought an acre in the cemetery, in which he placed her; and when the last was gone, he went back to his desolate home, to roll pills in agony, and to moisten his salts and senna with his tears !